THE ULTIMATE BUG FIELD GUIDE

THE ULTIMATE BUG FIELD GUIDE

13-Digit ISBN: 978-1-64643-338-4
10-Digit ISBN: 1-64643-338-6

This book may be ordered by mail from the publisher. Please include $5.99 for postage and handling. Please support your local bookseller first!

Books published by Cider Mill Press Book Publishers are available at special discounts for bulk purchases in the United States by corporations, institutions, and other organizations. For more information, please contact the publisher.

Applesauce Press is an imprint of
Cider Mill Press Book Publishers
"Where good books are ready for press"
PO Box 454
12 Spring Street
Kennebunkport, Maine 04046

Visit us online! cidermillpress.com

Typography: Matchwood, Flood, SS Nickson
Image credits: Images on pages 92-95 are used under official license from Shutterstock.com. All other images courtesy of Appleseed Press Book Publishers.

Printed in China

1 2 3 4 5 6 7 8 9 0

First Edition

THE ULTIMATE BUG

FIELD GUIDE

APPLESAUCE PRESS

KENNEBUNKPORT, MAINE

MY FIELD NOTES

Every good scientist needs a field guide. It's an essential tool for identifying wildlife and telling one species apart from another. Field guides are best used to learn about nature on the go while exploring. The pictures and descriptions they contain make it easier to know what you're looking at. And there are field guides for just about everything, including all kinds of plants, animals, and sea creatures. You can make your own field guide or add onto field guides just by taking notes about what you see when you look at different wildlife. What color is it? How big is it? Where did you find it? Knowing these details will help you recognize it when you see it again.

Bugs serve many roles. They are pollinators, decomposers, and recyclers. They are producers of silk, honey, beeswax, and various medicines. Bugs play a large part in the food chain, and serve as both predator and prey. Many birds, lizards, and other larger animals could not survive without bugs to feed on.

What does the word "bug" mean to you? We often refer to creepy-crawlies as bugs, but the word has many meanings.

In this field guide, the term "bug" means any arthropod (a small animal with jointed legs, a segmented body, and a hard exoskeleton). That includes insects, myriapods (millipedes and centipedes), and chelicerates (spiders, scorpions, and sea spiders).

Bugs are found all over the world, from the warm tropics to the frigid polar regions. They may be small, but they rule the Earth with their spectacular diversity. About 84% of all animals are arthropods! That includes more than a million named species of insects alone, and many more species await scientific description.

One thing that's true of all bugs is that we have a lot to learn about them. Whether it's through observations of bug behavior or scientific experiments, researchers continue to study bugs and their remarkable role on Earth. As you read through this field guide, keep your own notes and records about what you learn so you can become a true bug expert.

TWO LONG LEGS THAT LOOK LIKE FEATHERS

When threatened, this centipede shakes its back legs to make a hissing noise, like a rattlesnake.

FEMALES WILL PROTECT THEIR EGGS BY WAGGING THEIR BACK LEGS TO DISTRACT PREDATORS.

Sometimes, it causes the back section of their bodies to break off.

4-6 INCHES LONG (10-15 CENTIMETERS)

FEATHER-TAIL CENTIPEDE
(ALIPES GRANDIDIERI)

Found in eastern Africa

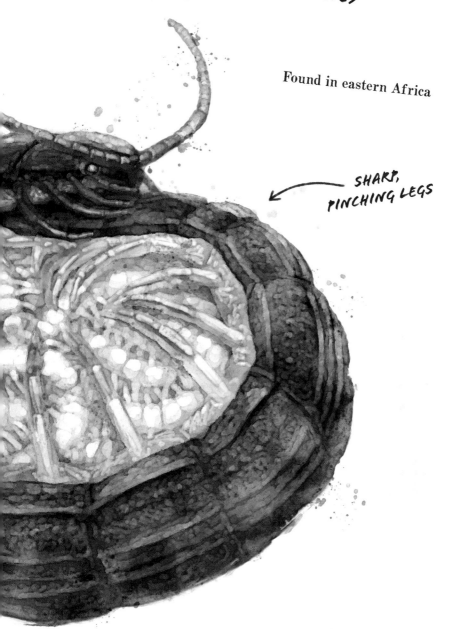

SHARP, PINCHING LEGS

COMMON EUROPEAN EARWIG

(FORFICULA AURICULARIA)

Found in North America,
Europe, and western Asia

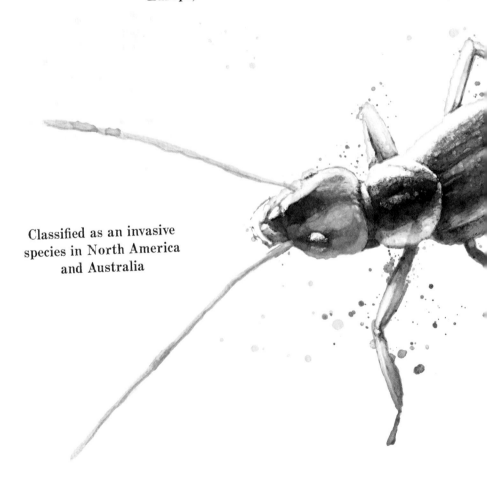

Classified as an invasive
species in North America
and Australia

←————————— 0.5 INCH LONG (1.3 CENTIMETERS) —

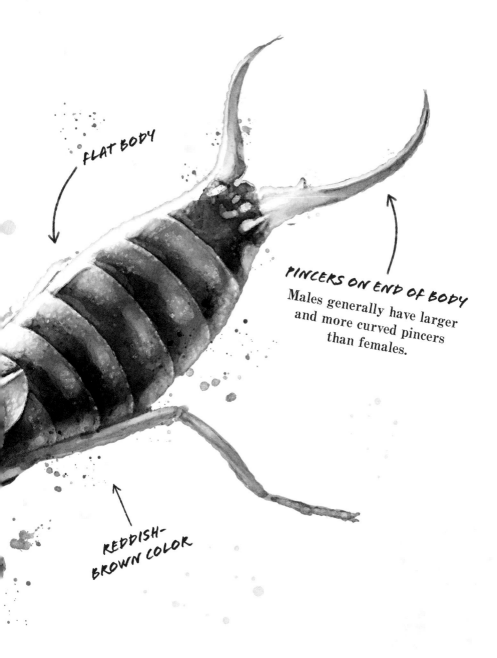

FLAT BODY

PINCERS ON END OF BODY
Males generally have larger and more curved pincers than females.

REDDISH-BROWN COLOR

They can get into floorboards, household plants, pantries, furniture, and clothing. The earwig mostly comes out at night, and takes shelter in dark, damp places.

The long tails of hair
are used like whips to
fight off predators.

LONG HAIRS ON THE
END OF THE BODY

LEAFLIKE
APPENDAGES ⟶

These leaflike parts
resemble the tail of
a peacock.

This mite is an herbivore, and
feeds on grasses and citrus fruits.

⟵————————— 0.01 INCH LONG (0.25 CENTIMETER) —

PEACOCK MITE
(TUCKERELLA JAPONICA)

Found in tropical climates

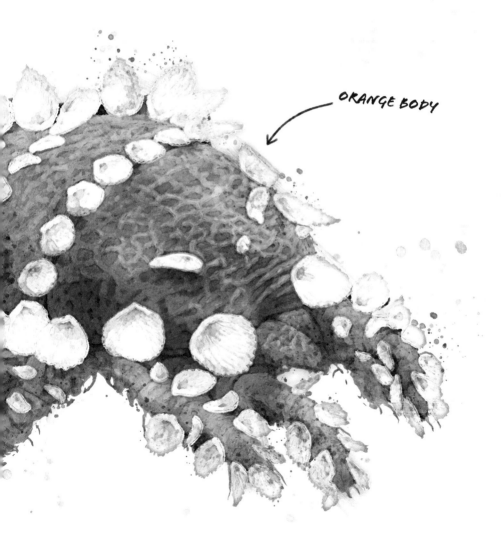

ORANGE BODY

This tarantula is critically endangered because it lives in only one forest reserve in Andhra Pradesh, India.

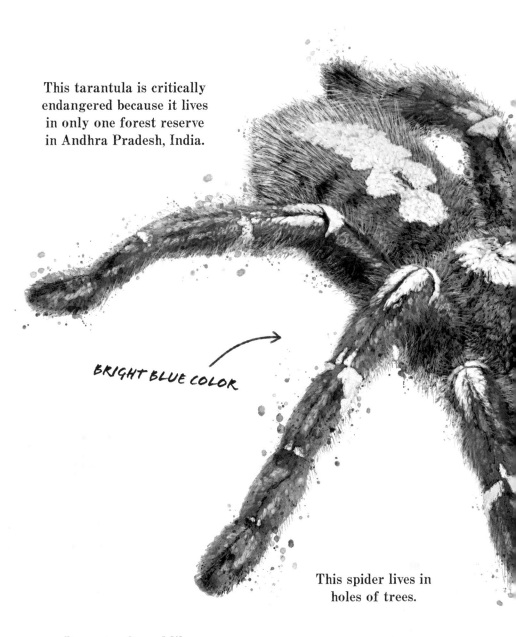

BRIGHT BLUE COLOR

This spider lives in holes of trees.

It creates funnel-like webs to catch its prey.

6- TO 8-INCH LEG SPAN (15-20 CENTIMETERS)

GOOTY SAPPHIRE TARANTULA

(POECILOTHERIA METALLICA)

COMMONLY KNOWN AS THE
"PEACOCK TARANTULA" OR
"METALLIC TARANTULA"

Found in central and
southern India

VENOMOUS FANGS

The fangs of an adult can
grow to be nearly 0.75 inch
long (1.9 centimeters).

GIANT PILL MILLIPEDE

(SPHAEROTHERIUM GIGANTEUM)

Found in southern and southeast Asia, southern Africa, and Australia

THIS BUG ROLLS INTO A BALL WHEN THREATENED. The tail wraps all the way around and covers its head.

When rolled up, it is about the size of a golf ball, but can be as big as a baseball.

This herbivore feeds on dead organic matter.

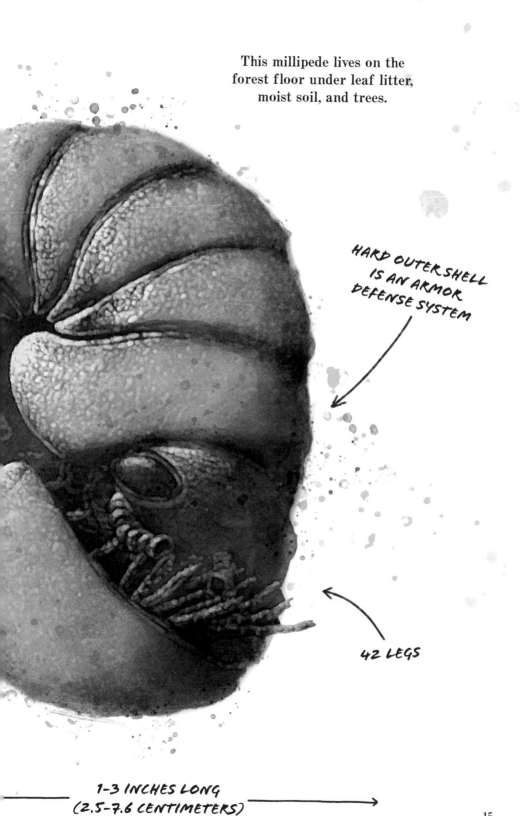

This millipede lives on the forest floor under leaf litter, moist soil, and trees.

HARD OUTER SHELL IS AN ARMOR DEFENSE SYSTEM

42 LEGS

1-3 INCHES LONG
(2.5-7.6 CENTIMETERS)

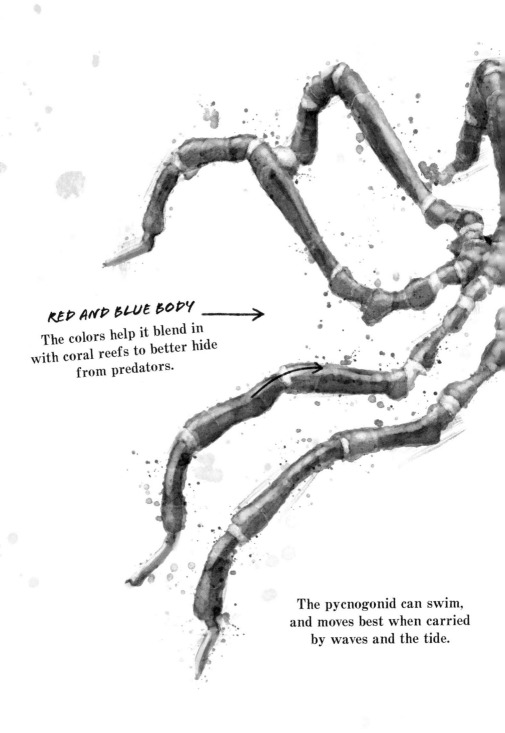

RED AND BLUE BODY ⟶

The colors help it blend in
with coral reefs to better hide
from predators.

The pycnogonid can swim,
and moves best when carried
by waves and the tide.

PYCNOGONID

(ANOPLODACTYLUS EVANSI)

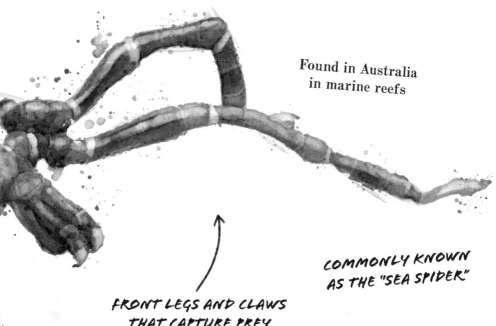

Found in Australia
in marine reefs

COMMONLY KNOWN
AS THE "SEA SPIDER"

FRONT LEGS AND CLAWS
THAT CAPTURE PREY

IT LIVES IN ROCK POOLS
AND ON CORAL REEFS.

It can survive about 52 feet
(16 meters) underwater.

← 0.4 INCH LONG (1 CENTIMETER) →

EMPEROR SCORPION

(PANDINUS IMPERATOR)

Found in western Africa

It lives in rain forests and savannas, and burrows into the soil beneath rocks and leaves.

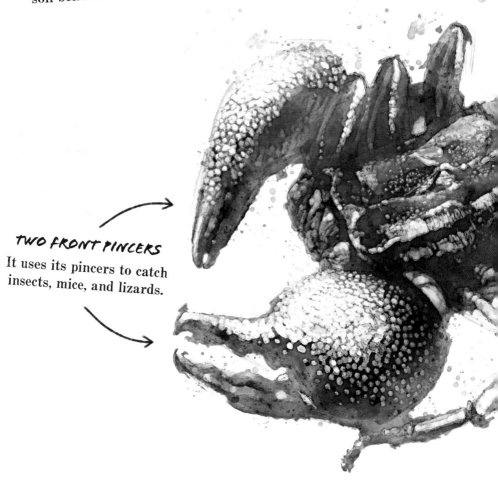

TWO FRONT PINCERS
It uses its pincers to catch insects, mice, and lizards.

LONG, CURVED TAIL
The tail has a special stinger filled with venom that paralyzes prey.

HARD, DARK, METALLIC BODY FOR PROTECTION

Its sting is fairly harmless to humans.

It glows under ultraviolet light.

— 8 INCHES LONG (20 CENTIMETERS) —→

19

IT WAGS ITS COLORFUL ABDOMEN FOR MATING DISPLAYS.

This spider has a unique mating dance in which it wiggles its body and raises and lowers its third pair of legs.

YELLOW AND RED MARKINGS

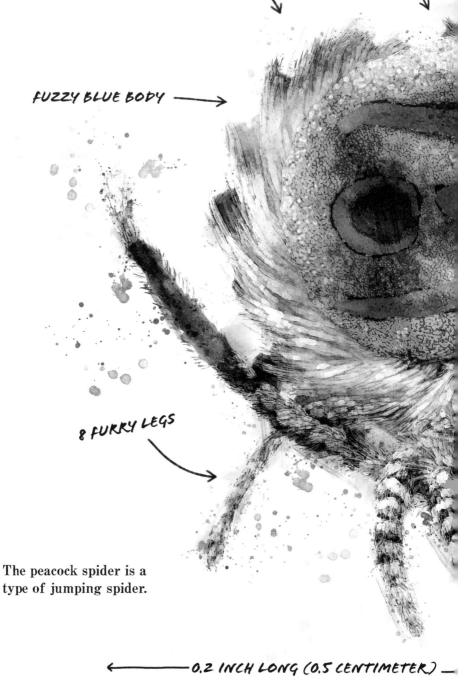

FUZZY BLUE BODY ⟶

8 FURRY LEGS

The peacock spider is a type of jumping spider.

⟵————0.2 INCH LONG (0.5 CENTIMETER) —

PEACOCK SPIDER

(MARATUS SPECIOSUS)

Found in Australia in the vegetation
on coastal sand dunes

ELONGATED THIRD
LEGS TIPPED WITH
WHITE BRUSHES

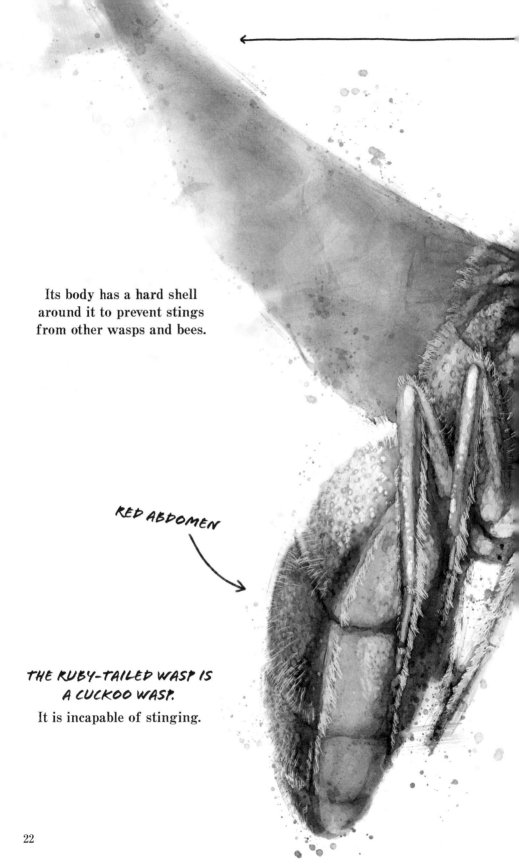

Its body has a hard shell around it to prevent stings from other wasps and bees.

RED ABDOMEN

THE RUBY-TAILED WASP IS A CUCKOO WASP.

It is incapable of stinging.

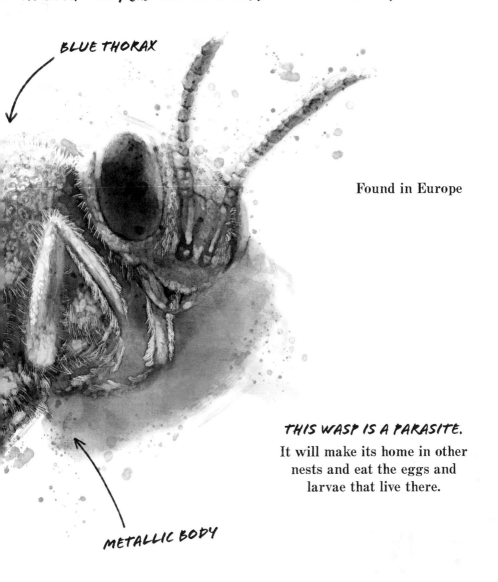

0.5 INCH LONG (1.3 CENTIMETERS)

BLUE THORAX

Found in Europe

THIS WASP IS A PARASITE.

It will make its home in other nests and eat the eggs and larvae that live there.

METALLIC BODY

RUBY-TAILED WASP

(CHRYSIS IGNITA)

METALLIC BLUE, GREEN, COPPER, OR GOLD BODY

Found in South America

HANSON'S ORCHID BEE

(EUGLOSSA HANSONI)

This bee is named after its
favorite food: the nectar of
orchid flowers.

Nectar gives it the energy
to fly long distances,
sometimes miles at a time,
to its next meal.

UNUSUALLY LONG TONGUE

Its tongue can reach into orchids
to eat the hidden nectar.

— 0.4-0.8 INCH LONG (1-2 CENTIMETERS) —————→

CRIMSON MARSH GLIDER

(TRITHEMIS AURORA)

Found in Asia

BRIGHT RED BODY
Males are bright red, while females have a yellow or brown body with black lines.

This common dragonfly is widely distributed and found throughout the year.

It lives mostly by marshes, ponds, or slow streams.

← ——————— 1 INCH LONG (2.54 CENTIMETERS) —

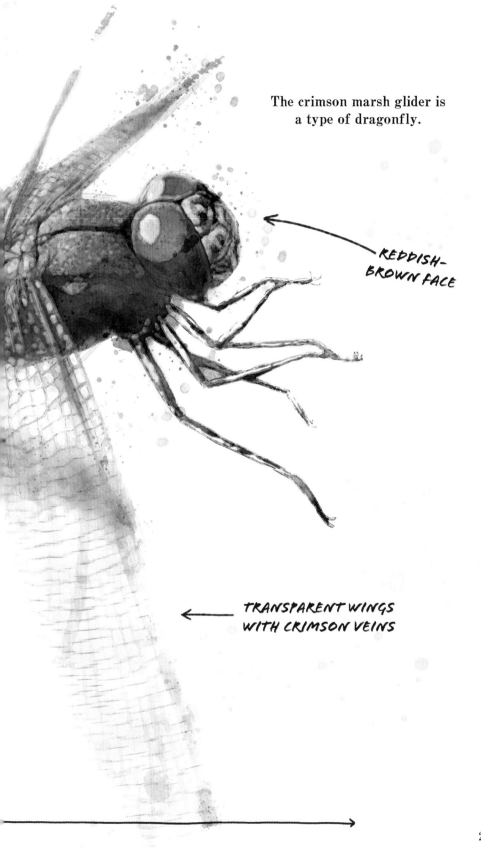

The crimson marsh glider is a type of dragonfly.

REDDISH-BROWN FACE

TRANSPARENT WINGS WITH CRIMSON VEINS

STRONG WINGS FOR MIGRATION

Every fall, monarchs migrate across North America to central Mexico to live out the winter months. They only live long enough to make the journey once in their lives, so it is unclear how the new butterflies know where to go each year.

WHITE SPOTS AROUND THE EDGES OF THE WINGS

MONARCH BUTTERFLY

(DANAUS PLEXIPPUS)

Found in North America
and Mexico

The monarch has a life cycle with
four stages: the egg, the larvae
(caterpillar), the pupa (chrysalis),
and the adult butterfly.

ORANGE WINGS WITH
BLACK VEINS

3- TO 4.7-INCH WINGSPAN
(8-12 CENTIMETERS)

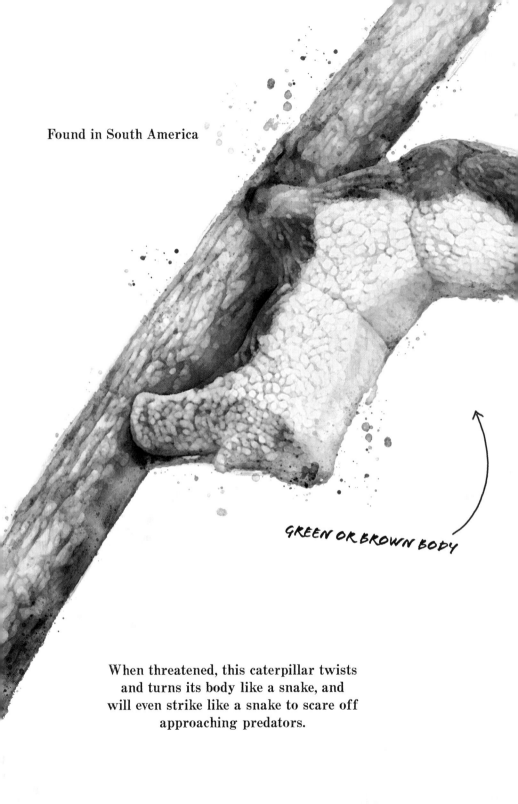

Found in South America

GREEN OR BROWN BODY

When threatened, this caterpillar twists
and turns its body like a snake, and
will even strike like a snake to scare off
approaching predators.

UP TO 4 INCHES LONG
(10 CENTIMETERS)

SNAKE-MIMICKING CATERPILLAR

(HEMEROPLANES TRIPTOLEMUS)

PATTERNED UNDERSIDE

WHITE SPOTS THAT
LOOK LIKE EYES

It inflates part of its
body to look like a
small snake.

TWO PAIRS OF HORNS

This caterpillar feeds on
tree sap and rotting fruit.

Found in Australia

TAILED EMPEROR BUTTERFLY CATERPILLAR

(POLYURA SEMPRONIUS)

2-3 INCHES LONG
(5-8 CENTIMETERS)

GREEN BODY
When fully mature, this caterpillar
becomes a black-and-white butterfly.

**CRESCENT-SHAPED
MARKINGS ON THE BACK**

**YELLOW LINE RUNNING
ALONG EACH SIDE OF
THE BODY**

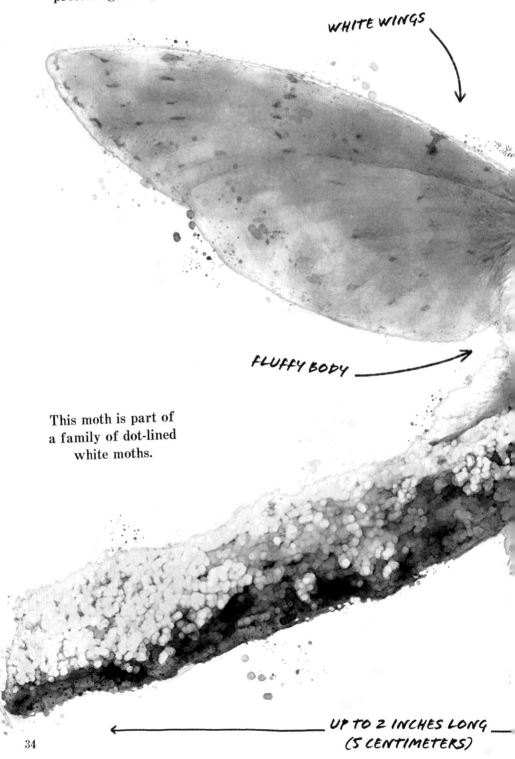

Its hairs can help it sense its environment, and protect against predators.

WHITE WINGS

FLUFFY BODY

This moth is part of a family of dot-lined white moths.

UP TO 2 INCHES LONG (5 CENTIMETERS)

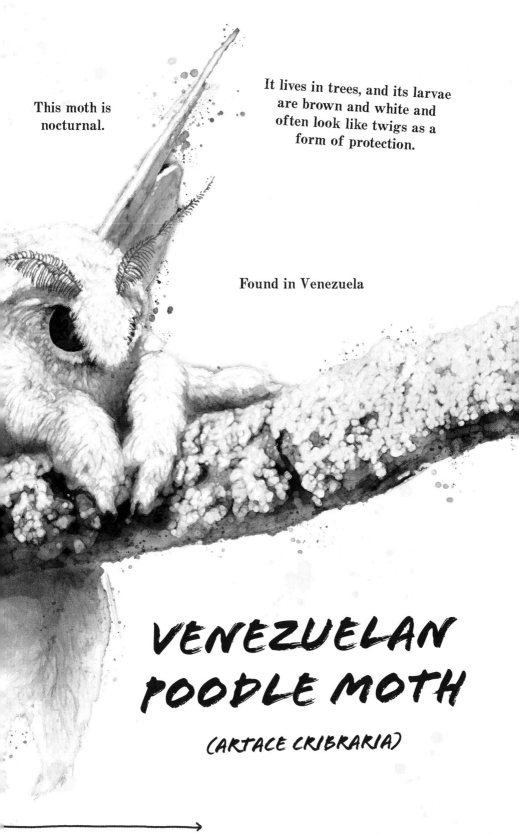

This moth is
nocturnal.

It lives in trees, and its larvae
are brown and white and
often look like twigs as a
form of protection.

Found in Venezuela

VENEZUELAN
POODLE MOTH
(ARTACE CRIBRARIA)

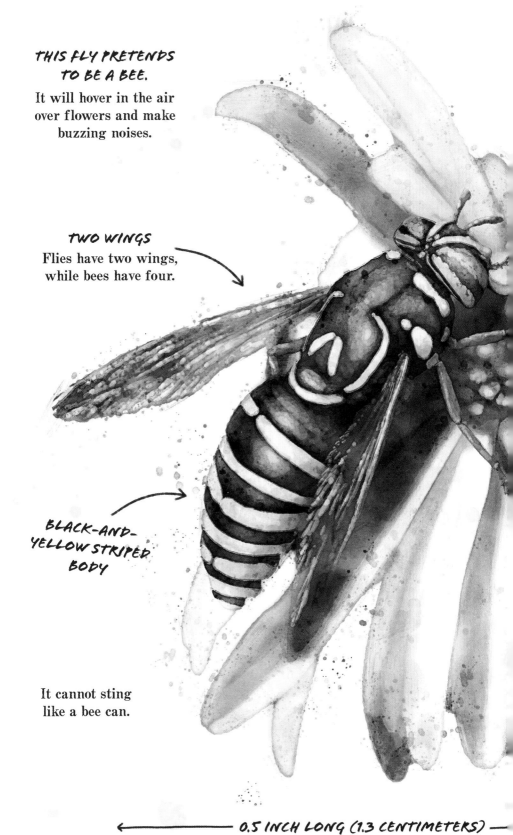

THIS FLY PRETENDS TO BE A BEE.

It will hover in the air over flowers and make buzzing noises.

TWO WINGS

Flies have two wings, while bees have four.

BLACK-AND-YELLOW STRIPED BODY

It cannot sting like a bee can.

0.5 INCH LONG (1.3 CENTIMETERS)

Its bee imitation tricks predators
into staying away.

SPILOMYIA FLY
(SPILOMYIA LONGICORNIS)

TRILOBITE BEETLE
(PLATERODRILUS PARADOXUS)

Found in India, southeast Asia, and other tropical areas

It eats fungi found in its tropical habitats.

SCALES OVER THE HEAD

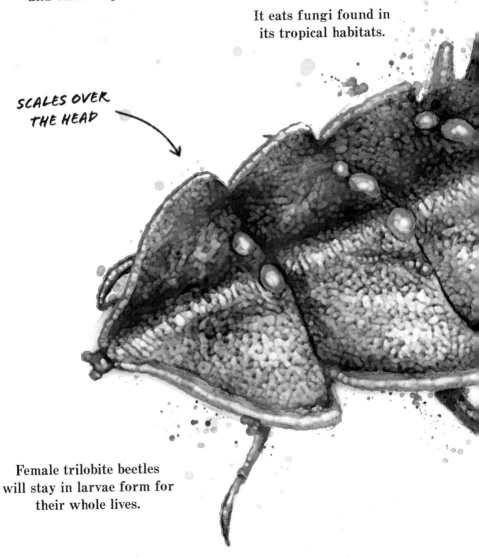

Female trilobite beetles will stay in larvae form for their whole lives.

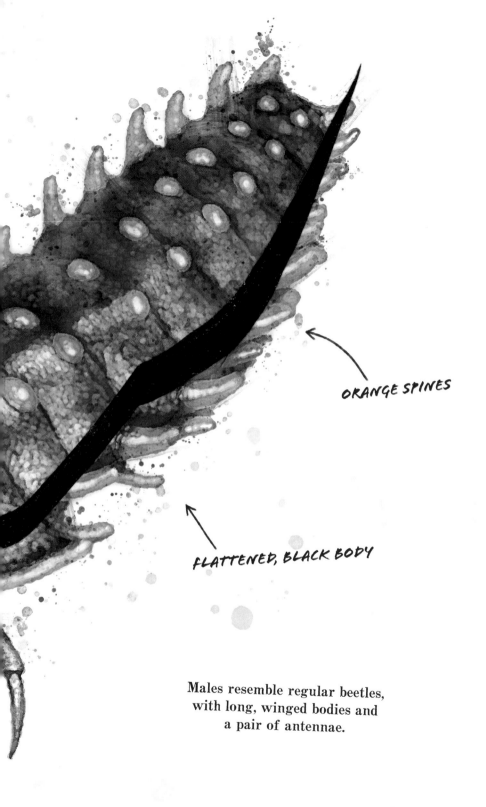

ORANGE SPINES

FLATTENED, BLACK BODY

Males resemble regular beetles,
with long, winged bodies and
a pair of antennae.

FEMALES 1.6-2.36 INCHES LONG (4-6 CENTIMETERS),
MALES 0.2-0.3 INCH LONG (0.5-0.8 CENTIMETER)

BLACK BODY WITH METALLIC BLUE AND ORANGE SPOTS

0.2–0.3 INCH LONG
(0.5–0.8 CENTIMETER)

POLKA-DOTTED CLOWN WEEVIL

(PACHYRRHYNCHUS ORBIFER)

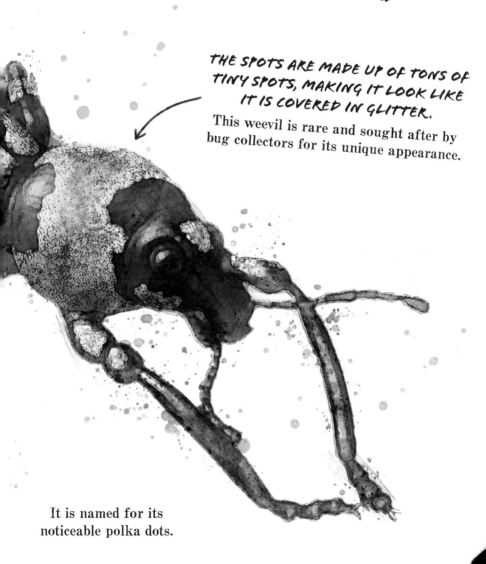

THE SPOTS ARE MADE UP OF TONS OF TINY SPOTS, MAKING IT LOOK LIKE IT IS COVERED IN GLITTER.

This weevil is rare and sought after by bug collectors for its unique appearance.

It is named for its noticeable polka dots.

BROWN BODY

Its main food is tree
sap and fruit common
to its habitat.

WINGS THAT STAY TUCKED
UNDERNEATH THE BODY
UNTIL NEEDED

BLACK HEAD WITH
WHITE STRIPES

MALES HAVE Y-SHAPED HORNS
AT THE ENDS OF THEIR HEADS.
They use this horn to fight other
Goliath beetles for food or mates.

The Goliath beetle is one of the
largest types of beetles, and can
grow to be as large as a small bird.

GOLIATH BEETLE

(GOLIATHUS GOLIATUS)

Found in Africa

RED DRIVER ANT

(DORYLUS HELVOLUS)

Found in Africa and parts of Asia

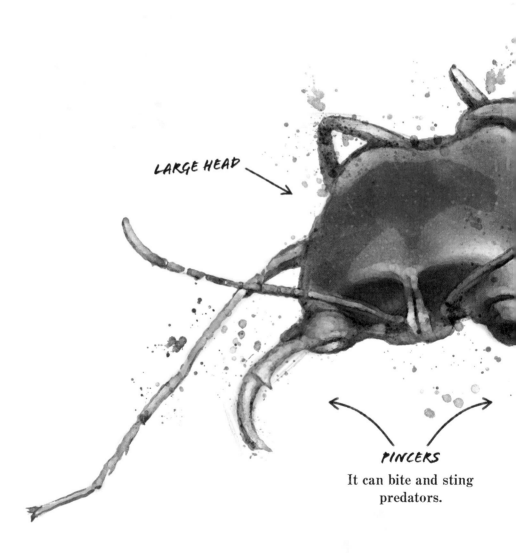

LARGE HEAD

PINCERS
It can bite and sting
predators.

This ant lives in colonies that can have millions of ants in one anthill.

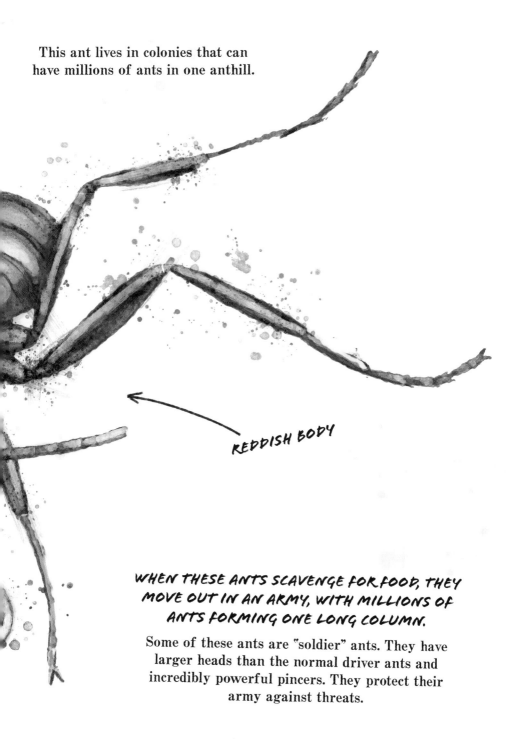

REDDISH BODY

WHEN THESE ANTS SCAVENGE FOR FOOD, THEY MOVE OUT IN AN ARMY, WITH MILLIONS OF ANTS FORMING ONE LONG COLUMN.

Some of these ants are "soldier" ants. They have larger heads than the normal driver ants and incredibly powerful pincers. They protect their army against threats.

0.08–0.3 INCH LONG
(0.2–0.8 CENTIMETER)

GIRAFFE WEEVIL

(TRACHELOPHORUS GIRAFFA)

Found in Madagascar

RED BODY →

A male's neck can be two to three times longer than a female's. Its neck is used for fighting and building nests.

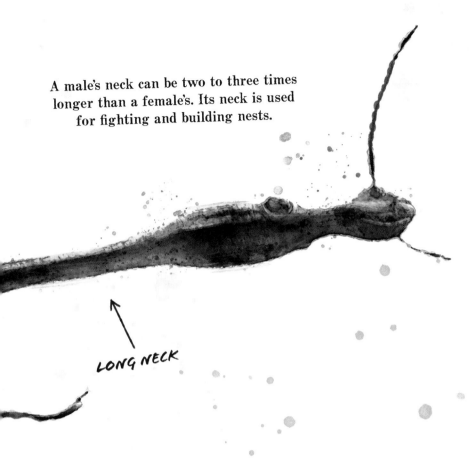

LONG NECK

This weevil is named after the giraffe for its long neck.

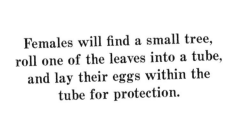

Females will find a small tree, roll one of the leaves into a tube, and lay their eggs within the tube for protection.

— 0.8 INCH LONG (2 CENTIMETERS) ⟶

LARGE HIND LEGS
Only the males have
frog-like legs.

Its legs help it cling to branches and win
wrestling matches against other males.
It will wiggle its back legs at another
beetle in threat of an attack.

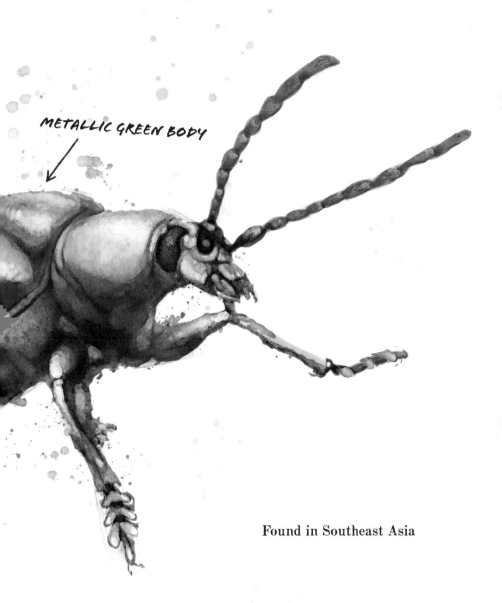

METALLIC GREEN BODY

Found in Southeast Asia

FROG-LEGGED BEETLE

(SAGRA BUQUETI)

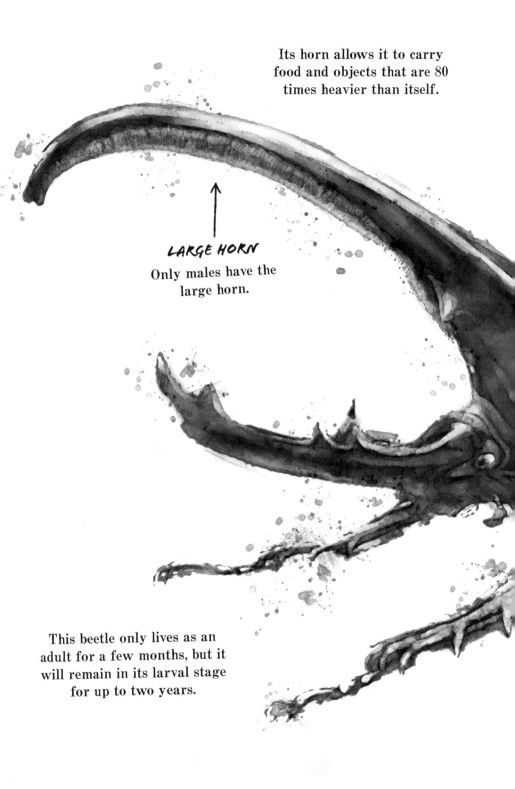

Its horn allows it to carry food and objects that are 80 times heavier than itself.

LARGE HORN
Only males have the large horn.

This beetle only lives as an adult for a few months, but it will remain in its larval stage for up to two years.

←———— 2.75–7 INCHES LONG (7–18 CENTIMETERS) ·

HERCULES BEETLE
(DYNASTES HERCULES)

Found in Central and
South America

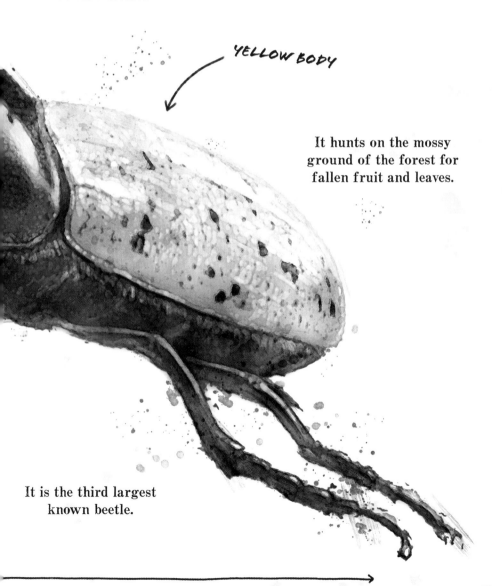

YELLOW BODY

It hunts on the mossy
ground of the forest for
fallen fruit and leaves.

It is the third largest
known beetle.

SPINY FLOWER MANTIS

(PSEUDOCREOBOTRA WAHLBERGII)

Found in southern and
eastern Africa

It camouflages itself as a
flower to lure prey.

When a threat approaches, the spiny flower
mantis raises its wings to show their spiral
markings and startle the predator. The
mantis tricks it into believing it's much
larger than it really is.

BEIGE BODY WITH GREEN,
ORANGE, AND BROWN
MARKINGS IN A
SWIRL PATTERN

This mantis will not chase after
food. It will wait completely still
for prey to pass by.

LARGE EYESPOTS
ON WINGS

1-2 INCHES LONG
(2.54-5 CENTIMETERS)

BROWN OR GREEN BODY

IT REMAINS ABSOLUTELY MOTIONLESS, IMITATING A FLOWER, UNTIL ITS PREY TRIES TO LAND. THEN, IT QUICKLY STRIKES.

Its hunting strategy allows it to feed on other airborne insects that would be too hard to catch otherwise.

DEVIL'S FLOWER MANTIS

(IDOLOMANTIS DIABOLICA)

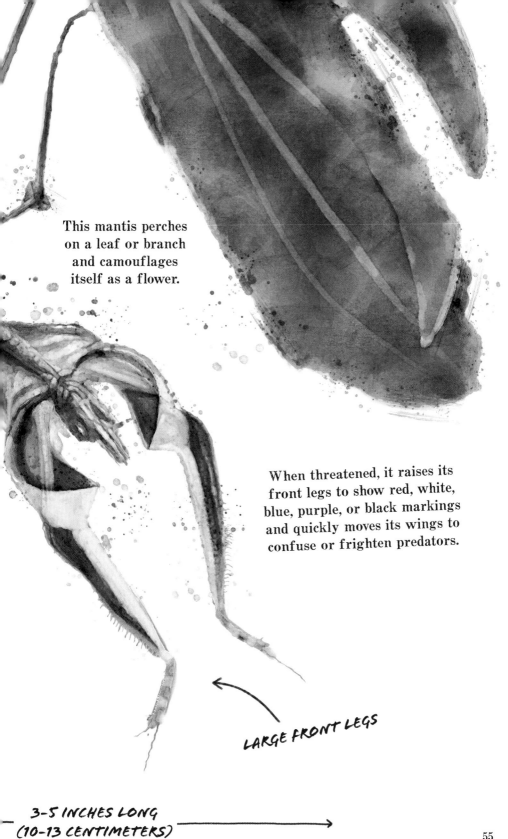

This mantis perches on a leaf or branch and camouflages itself as a flower.

When threatened, it raises its front legs to show red, white, blue, purple, or black markings and quickly moves its wings to confuse or frighten predators.

LARGE FRONT LEGS

3-5 INCHES LONG
(10-13 CENTIMETERS)

MOSS MIMIC STICK INSECT
(TRYCHOPEPLUS LACINIATUS)

Found in Costa Rica and other tropical regions

When it stays still, it looks like a stick.

ITS UNIQUE CAMOUFLAGE HELPS IT BLEND INTO TREES AND MOSS.

This is a great defense against predators, and helps keep it safe.

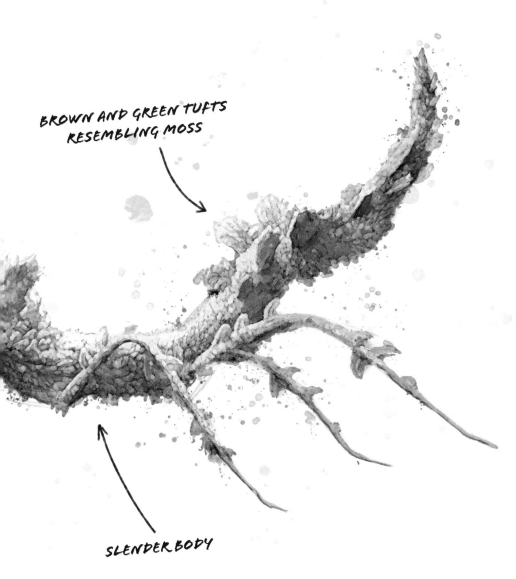

BROWN AND GREEN TUFTS RESEMBLING MOSS

SLENDER BODY

—2-3 INCHES LONG (4-8 CENTIMETERS) —————→

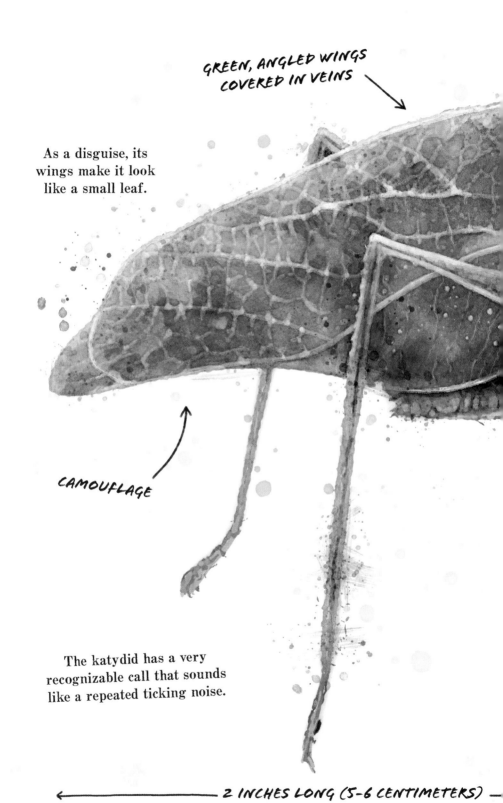

GREEN, ANGLED WINGS
COVERED IN VEINS

As a disguise, its
wings make it look
like a small leaf.

CAMOUFLAGE

The katydid has a very
recognizable call that sounds
like a repeated ticking noise.

2 INCHES LONG (5-6 CENTIMETERS)

It likes shade, and is found in forests or areas with lots of leaves and shrubs.

Found in the southwestern and eastern United States

BROAD-WINGED KATYDID
(MICROCENTRUM RHOMBIFOLIUM)

It feeds on bugs known
as plant lice, which can be
harmful to plants and crops.

REDDISH OR ORANGEISH
BODY WITH BLACK SPOTS

This beetle is one of the most
varied species in the world, and has
a wide range of color forms.

Found in Asia, North America,
South America, Europe, and
South Africa

It releases a smell and
fluid when frightened
to scare off predators.

The ladybeetle often
invades homes in the
winter to hibernate.

COMMONLY
KNOWN AS THE
"LADYBUG"

HARLEQUIN LADYBEETLE

(HARMONIA AXYRIDIS)

COMMON
EASTERN FIREFLY
(PHOTINUS PYRALIS)

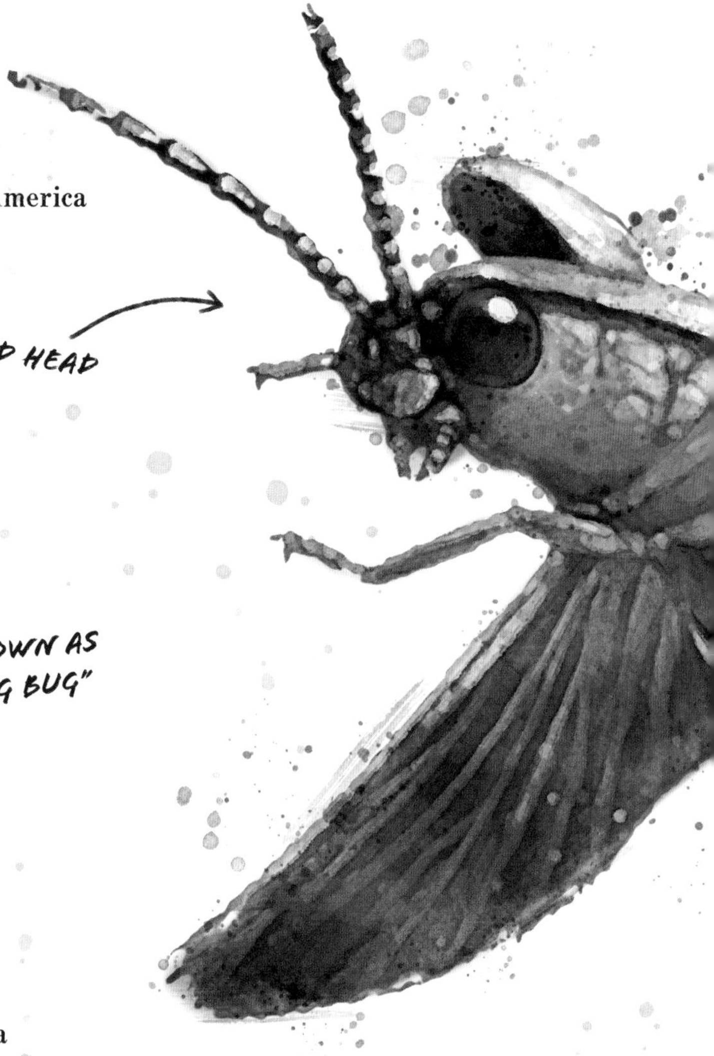

Found in North America

RED HEAD

COMMONLY KNOWN AS
THE "LIGHTNING BUG"

Fireflies release a
bad smell or a sticky
substance when a
predator attacks.

IT USES A SPECIAL ORGAN ON THE LOWER PART OF ITS BODY TO FLASH LIGHT PATTERNS.

These patterns help other fireflies find one another at night.

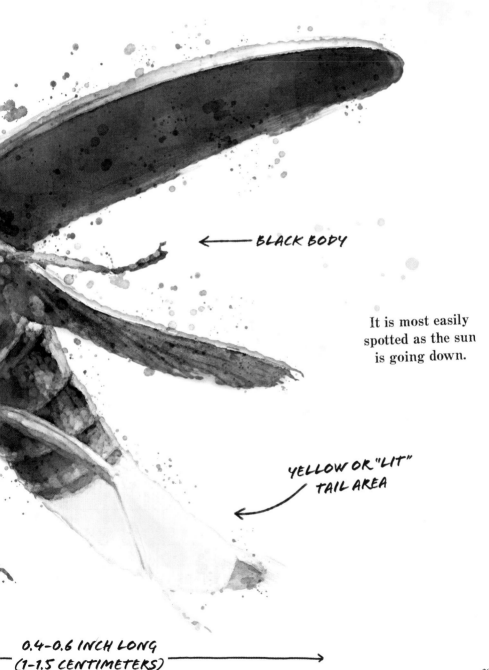

←———— BLACK BODY

It is most easily spotted as the sun is going down.

YELLOW OR "LIT" TAIL AREA

0.4–0.6 INCH LONG (1–1.5 CENTIMETERS)

LEICHHARDT'S GRASSHOPPER
(PETASIDA EPHIPPIGERA)

Found in Australia

ORANGE BODY
WITH BLACK SPOTS

It comes out in October every year during the first rains of the monsoon season.

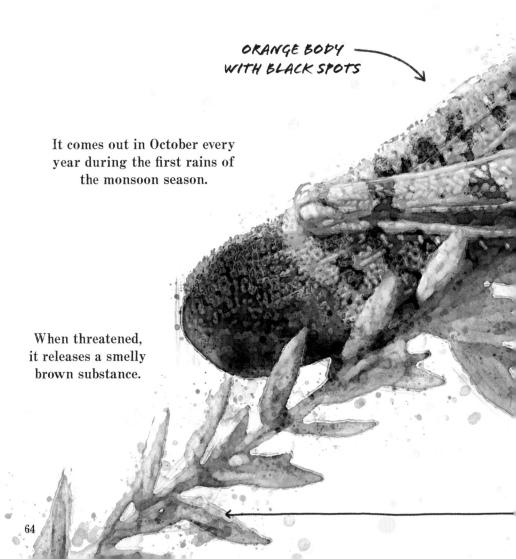

When threatened, it releases a smelly brown substance.

BLUE PATCHES ON HEAD AND THORAX

This grasshopper will often live on just one bush for its entire life.

IT PREFERS TO EAT A MINTY-SMELLING BUT BITTER-TASTING PLANT CALLED PITYRODIA.

Thanks to the bitter taste of the pityrodia bush, this grasshopper tastes terrible, and is less likely to become prey.

2-2.5 INCHES LONG (5-7 CENTIMETERS)

Its feather-like tail is used
to distract approaching
predators, and may even
trick them into attacking the
moving tail while the insect
escapes unharmed.

LONG, FRINGE-LIKE TAIL

ROOSTER TAIL CICADA

(LYSTRA LANATA)

Found in tropical regions,
particularly in South America

BLACK SPECKLED BODY

RED SIDES OF HEAD

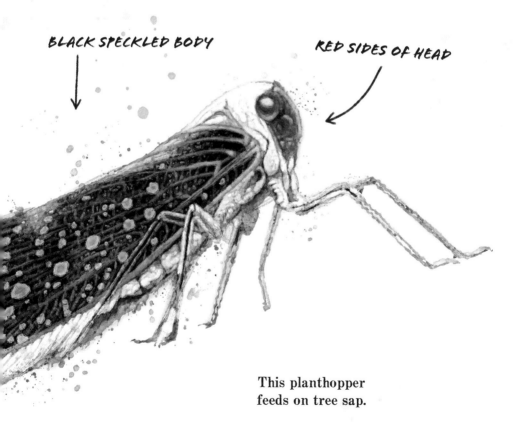

This planthopper
feeds on tree sap.

1 INCH LONG (2.54 CENTIMETERS)

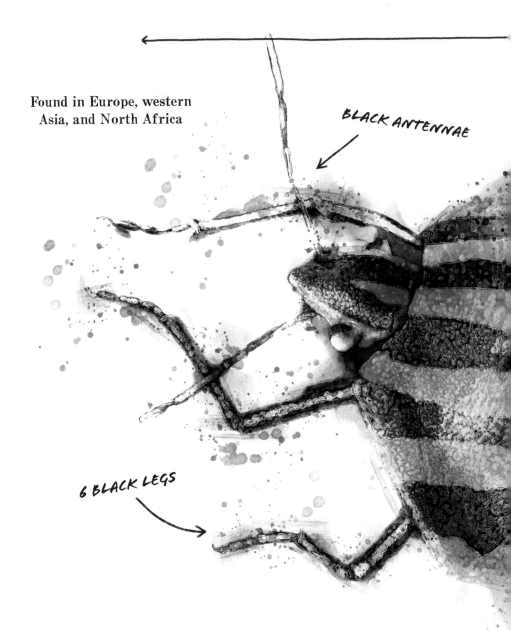

Found in Europe, western
Asia, and North Africa

BLACK ANTENNAE

6 BLACK LEGS

RED-AND-BLACK
STRIPED STINK BUG
(GRAPHOSOMA LINEATUM)

0.3–0.5 INCH LONG
(0.76–1.3 CENTIMETERS)

RED AND BLACK STRIPES ON THE BODY
The pronotum has 6 black bands.

The exoskeleton of this stink bug's body acts as a shield.

Its colors warn predators that it doesn't taste good.

SIDES OF THE ABDOMINAL SEGMENTS ARE RED WITH SMALL BLACK SPOTS

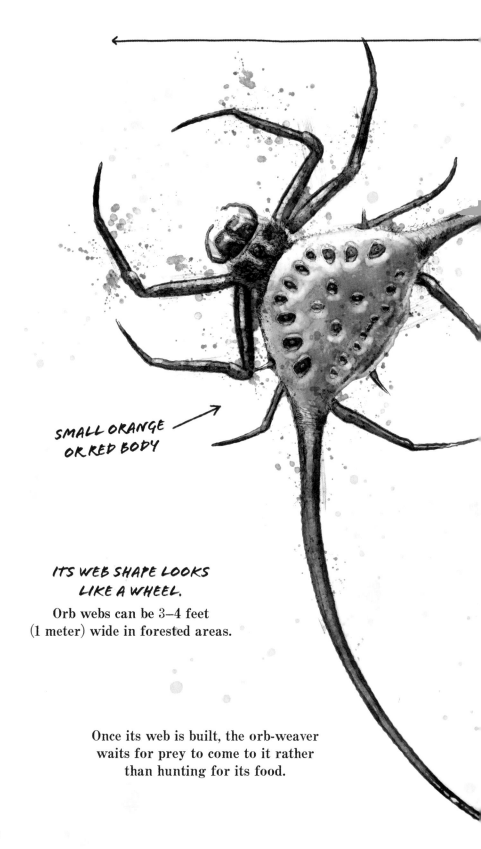

SMALL ORANGE
OR RED BODY

ITS WEB SHAPE LOOKS
LIKE A WHEEL.

Orb webs can be 3–4 feet
(1 meter) wide in forested areas.

Once its web is built, the orb-weaver
waits for prey to come to it rather
than hunting for its food.

These spines protect this
spider from predators.

Males are significantly
smaller than females, and
have stout, conical spines.

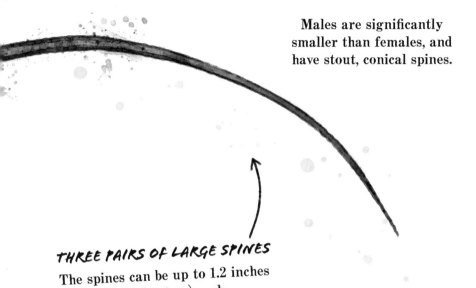

THREE PAIRS OF LARGE SPINES
The spines can be up to 1.2 inches
(3 centimeters) each.

Females have tough,
shell-like abdomens.

Found in Southeast Asia

SPINY ORB-WEAVER
(MACRACANTHA ARCUATA)

MEMBRACID

(CLADONOTA BENITEZ)

Found in South America

COMMONLY KNOWN AS A "TREEHOPPER"

It hops between trees in the forest.

CRESCENT-SHAPED BODY

The crescent shape and the treehopper's colors help it camouflage into its habitat.

Treehoppers have specialized hind limb muscles that help them jump very far.

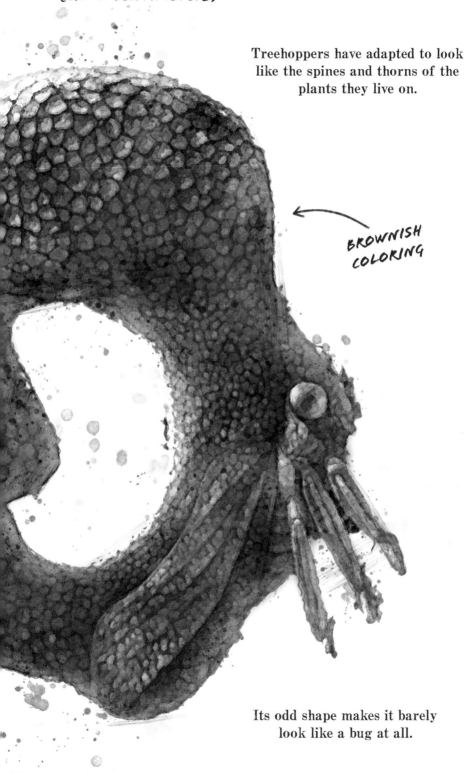

**0.08–0.8 INCH LONG
(0.2–2 CENTIMETERS)** →

Treehoppers have adapted to look
like the spines and thorns of the
plants they live on.

← BROWNISH
COLORING

Its odd shape makes it barely
look like a bug at all.

BLUE, BLACK, AND WHITE MARKINGS THAT LOOK LIKE A FACE

YELLOW BODY

THIS RARE GIANT SHIELD BUG IS A TYPE OF STINK BUG.

It sprays a bad-smelling liquid from its body when threatened.

0.2–0.7 INCH LONG
(0.5–1.8 CENTIMETERS)

MAN-FACED STINK BUG

(CATACANTHUS INCARNATUS)

Found in Southeast Asia

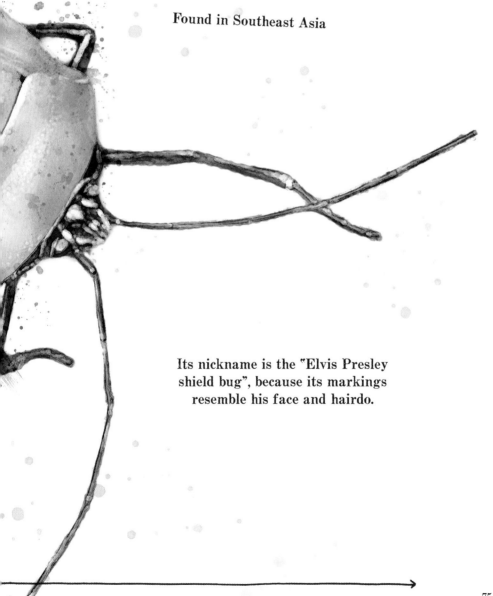

Its nickname is the "Elvis Presley shield bug", because its markings resemble his face and hairdo.

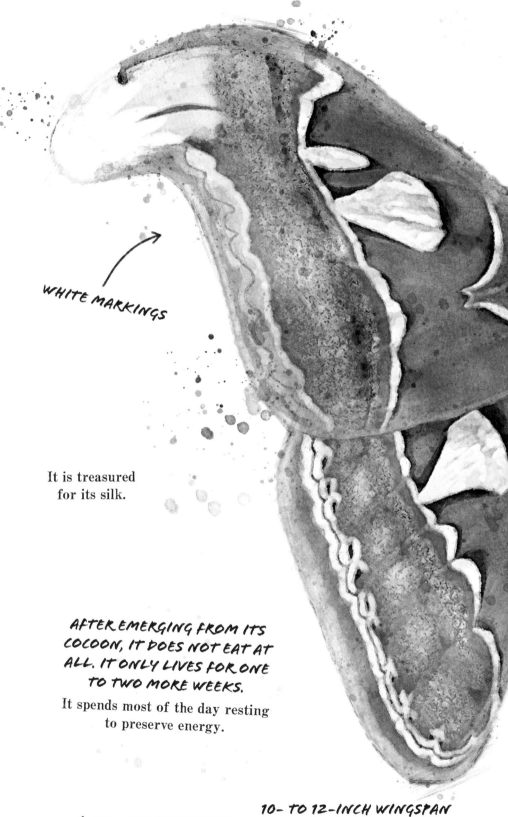

WHITE MARKINGS

It is treasured
for its silk.

AFTER EMERGING FROM ITS
COCOON, IT DOES NOT EAT AT
ALL. IT ONLY LIVES FOR ONE
TO TWO MORE WEEKS.

It spends most of the day resting
to preserve energy.

10- TO 12-INCH WINGSPAN
(25-30 CENTIMETERS)

GIANT ATLAS MOTH
(ATTACUS ATLAS)

This moth is named after the Greek god Atlas.

Found in Southeast Asia

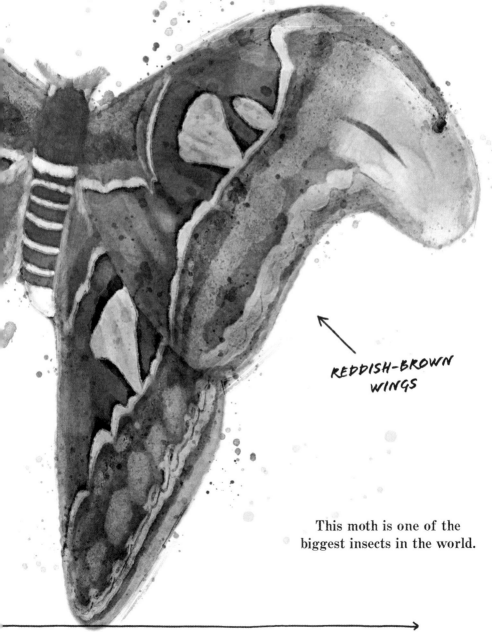

REDDISH-BROWN WINGS

This moth is one of the biggest insects in the world.

ASSASSIN BUG

(ACANTHASPIS PETAX)

Found in East Africa and Malaysia

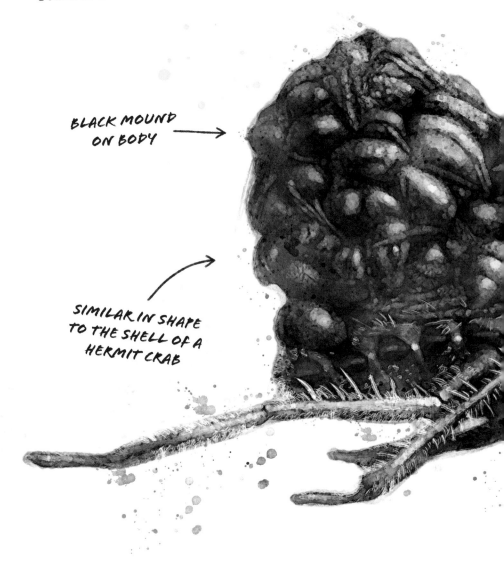

BLACK MOUND ON BODY →

↗ SIMILAR IN SHAPE TO THE SHELL OF A HERMIT CRAB

← ——— 0.5 INCH LONG (1.3 CENTIMETERS) ———

With prey on its back, it is unrecognizable to the spiders that would normally try to hunt it.

IT HUNTS ANTS AS FOOD, THEN USES STICKY SALIVA TO ADD THE ANT CORPSES TO THE MOUND OF BODIES ON ITS BACK.

This tricks predators into thinking this bug is larger than it is.

It is part of a family
called planthoppers.

Found in Southeast Asia

GREEN SPOTTED OR
STRIPED WINGS

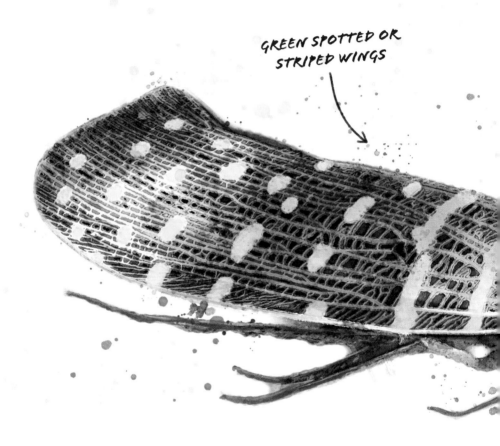

Its large mouth allows it to better get
into plants and trees to find food.

←———————— 3 INCHES LONG (7.6 CENTIMETERS) ———

LANTERN BUG
(PYROPS INTRICATUS)

THE LANTERN BUG DOESN'T ACTUALLY LIGHT UP.

It got its name because its wings are reflective.

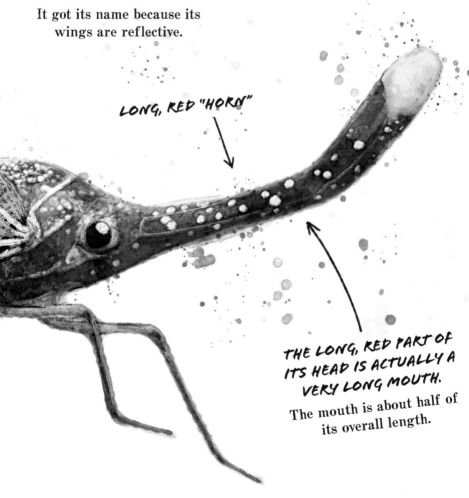

LONG, RED "HORN"

THE LONG, RED PART OF ITS HEAD IS ACTUALLY A VERY LONG MOUTH.

The mouth is about half of its overall length.

It releases a slimy substance to fight off predators.

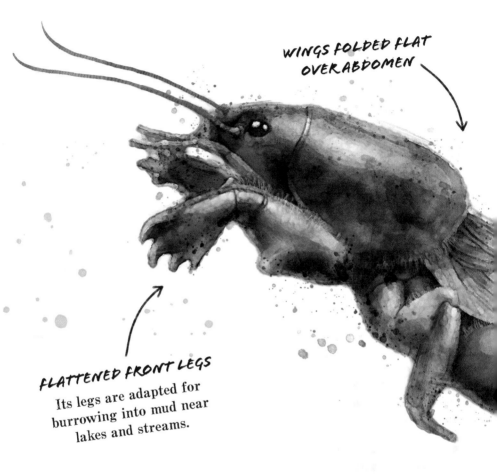

WINGS FOLDED FLAT OVER ABDOMEN

FLATTENED FRONT LEGS
Its legs are adapted for burrowing into mud near lakes and streams.

NORTHERN MOLE CRICKET
(NEOCURTILLA HEXADACTYLA)

It spends most of its life
underground, but adults have
wings that they use to disperse
for breeding season.

This cricket has a low-
pitched chirp and will call
from its burrow.

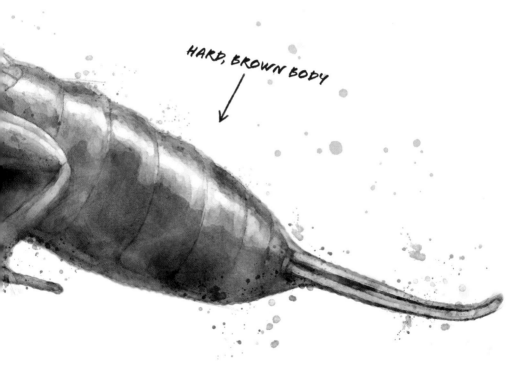

HARD, BROWN BODY

Found in eastern North America

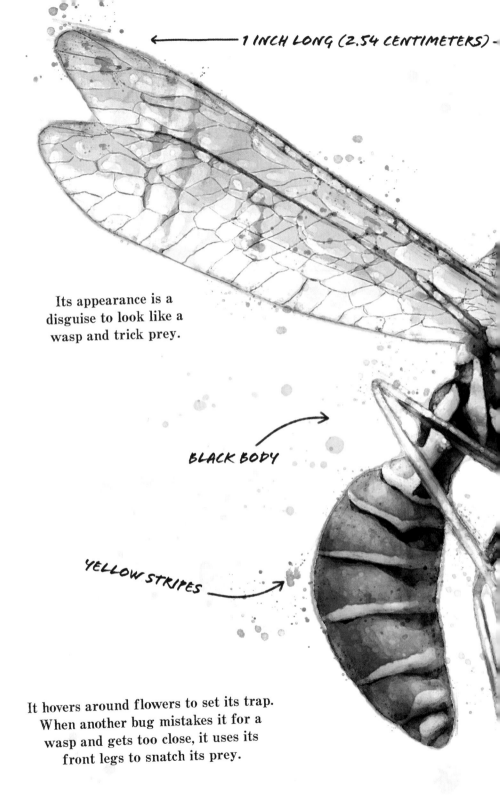

1 INCH LONG (2.54 CENTIMETERS)

Its appearance is a disguise to look like a wasp and trick prey.

BLACK BODY

YELLOW STRIPES

It hovers around flowers to set its trap. When another bug mistakes it for a wasp and gets too close, it uses its front legs to snatch its prey.

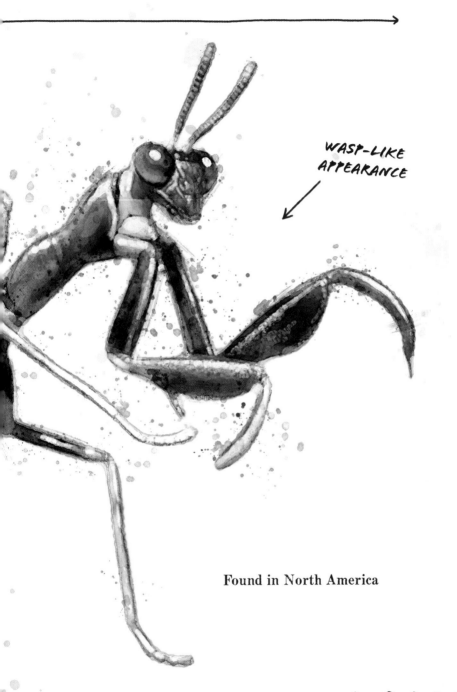

WASP-LIKE
APPEARANCE

Found in North America

WASP MANTIDFLY

(CLIMACIELLA BRUNNEA)

It will live close to weaver ant
colonies and pretend to be part
of the colony to look for prey.

This spider impersonates
the weaver ant.

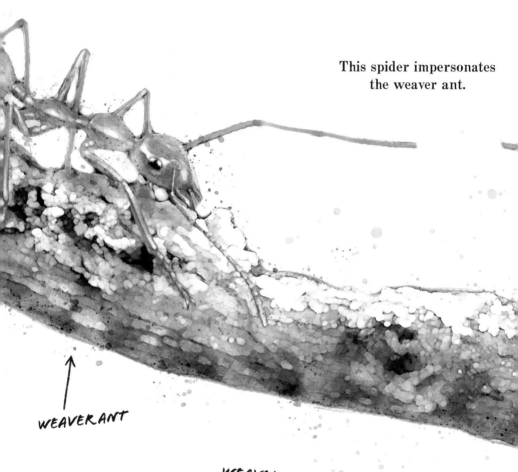

WEAVER ANT

WEAVER ANTS ONLY HAVE SIX LEGS,
BUT THIS SPIDER HAS EIGHT.
It will raise its front two legs to create
fake antennae to complete the disguise.

WEAVER ANT-MIMICKING JUMPING SPIDER

(MYRMARACHNE SMARAGDINA)

Found in Southeast
Asia and Australia

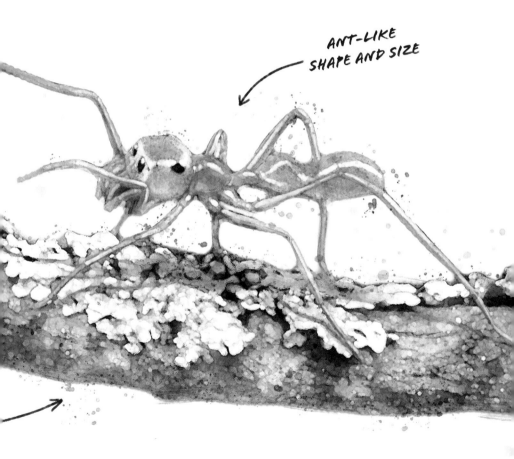

ANT-LIKE
SHAPE AND SIZE

0.25 INCH LONG
(0.6 CENTIMETER)

FAIRYFLY WASP

(KIKIKI HUNA)

Found in Hawaii,
Costa Rica, and Trinidad

BLACK, YELLOW,
OR BROWN BODY

It has a lifespan of
only a few days.

LONG, CLUB-LIKE
ANTENNAE

LESS THAN 0.2 MILLIMETER LONG

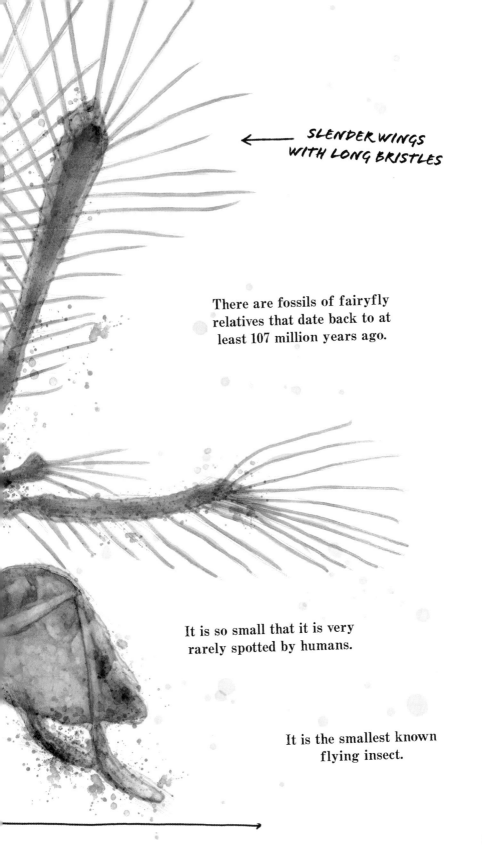

SLENDER WINGS
WITH LONG BRISTLES

There are fossils of fairyfly
relatives that date back to at
least 107 million years ago.

It is so small that it is very
rarely spotted by humans.

It is the smallest known
flying insect.

TIGER BEETLE

(CICINDELA AURULENTA)

Found in China,
Thailand, and Malaysia

STRONG, PINCER-
LIKE MOUTH

COMMONLY KNOWN AS
THE "GOLDEN-SPOTTED
TIGER BEETLE"

BLUE BODY WITH
RED STRIPE

It is an incredibly fast
runner, and is known as a
fierce predator.

WHITE OR YELLOW SPOTS

Sometimes it runs so quickly
it can't see, and it has to stop
in order to get its bearings.

0.6–0.7 INCH LONG
(1.5–1.8 CENTIMETERS)

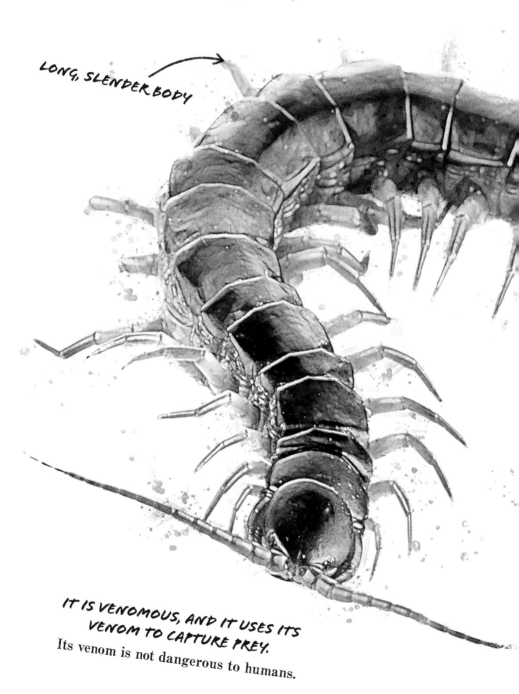

10-12 INCHES LONG
(26-30 CENTIMETERS)

The giant centipede is the
largest centipede in the world.

LONG, SLENDER BODY

IT IS VENOMOUS, AND IT USES ITS
VENOM TO CAPTURE PREY.
Its venom is not dangerous to humans.

Found in South America
and the Caribbean

COMMONLY KNOWN AS THE
"PERUVIAN GIANT YELLOW-LEG
CENTIPEDE" OR "AMAZONIAN
GIANT CENTIPEDE"

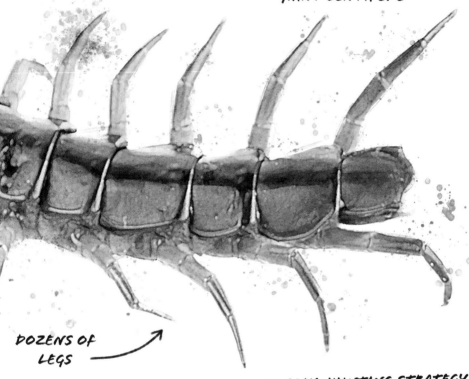

DOZENS OF
LEGS

UNIQUE HUNTING STRATEGY

It will crawl to the ceiling of
caves, hang from its back sets of
legs, and wait for a passing bat
to get close enough to catch.

It is a carnivore, and its size
allows it to prey on insects,
lizards, frogs, small birds,
mice, and even bats.

GIANT CENTIPEDE

(SCOLOPENDRA GIGANTEA)

RAINBOW DUNG BEETLE

(PHANAEUS VINDEX)

It is part of a family called scarab beetles, which were worshipped in ancient Egypt.

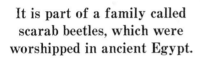 YELLOW, RED, AND COPPER-COLORED THORAX

METALLIC GREEN ABDOMEN

Found in North America

0.4-0.8 INCH LONG (1-2 CENTIMETERS)

It will tunnel under a pile of dung to lay its eggs, hence the "dung" part of its name.

It plays an important role in reducing waste in the environment by moving excrement.

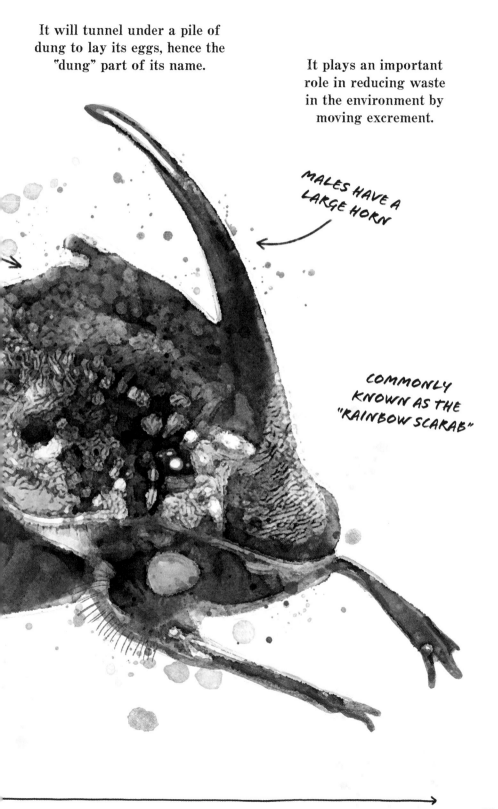

MALES HAVE A LARGE HORN

COMMONLY KNOWN AS THE "RAINBOW SCARAB"

ABOUT APPLESAUCE PRESS BOOK PUBLISHERS

Good ideas ripen with time. From seed to harvest, Applesauce Press crafts books with beautiful designs, creative formats, and kid-friendly information on a variety of topics. Like our parent company, Cider Mill Press Book Publishers, our press bears fruit twice a year, publishing a new crop of titles each spring and fall.

"Where Good Books Are Ready for Press"

VISIT US ONLINE
cidermillpress.com

OR WRITE TO US AT
PO Box 454
12 Spring Street
Kennebunkport, Maine 04046

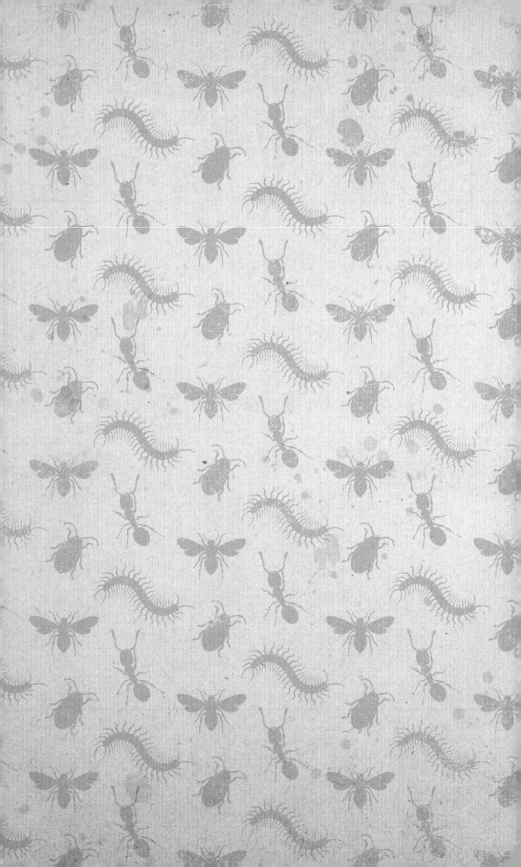